FLAMINGOS

FLAMINGOS

DON PATTON

THE CHILD'S WORLD

You are standing on the shore of a large, shallow lake that seems to be covered by a brilliant pink color. When you look more closely, though, the color seems to move! A loud, gooselike call echoes from the lake. As a truck rolls up to the shore, the mass of pink explodes into the air. First hundreds, then thousands of pink flamingos take to the air in a dazzling wave of color. They fly to the opposite shore, where they land and slowly begin to feed.

Flamingos are very particular about the types of areas, called *habitats*, in which they will live. They prefer shallow, very salty lagoons or lakes. They are very easily disturbed and usually choose large bodies of water so they can feed and breed in privacy.

The *greater flamingo* lives in many locations throughout the world—in North and West Africa, South America, southern Europe and Russia, and India. The *lesser flamingo* is found in the Rift Valley of East Africa, and in southern Africa and northwestern India. The *Caribbean flamingo* lives in the West Indies, a group of islands in the Caribbean Sea. A small colony of Caribbean flamingos also lives in the Galapagos Islands, northwest of South America in the Pacific Ocean. Finally, the *Andean flamingo* and *James's flamingo* are found in the high Andes Mountains of western South America.

To feed, the flamingo must dip its downturned bill upside down into the water. Its bill is adapted to strain small food particles from the water. The flamingo creates suction by opening its bill slightly and moving its tongue back toward its throat. This suction forces water through a coarse filter made of bony plates and into the flamingo's mouth. The coarse filter screens out large particles.

The flamingo then closes its bill and pushes its tongue forward, forcing the water through a fine bony filter. Small food items such as algae, small clams and shrimp, tiny insects, and even microscopic animals called *protozoa* are strained from the water and wet mud.

The algae captured during feeding contain chemicals known as *carotenoids*. These chemicals are responsible for the flamingo's beautiful pink color. Carotenoids are also found in some foods that we commonly eat, such as carrots—but luckily, we don't turn a bright pink!

To ensure that the entire colony breeds at the same time, flamingos have developed beautiful group dances called *breeding displays*. These dances start slowly, with just a few birds dancing, and then gradually build until the entire colony participates. In *head-flagging*, the first part of its display, each flamingo stretches its neck high toward the sky. This is followed by *wing-saluting*, in which the animal holds its head high and stretches, then folds its wings, showing a brilliant flash of black against pink as the black wingtips are quickly displayed. Finally, the flamingo performs a *twist-preen*, in which it twists its neck under an outstretched wing and smoothes its feathers with its bill. Group displays may occur off and on for months before the flamingos finally select mates.

Once mates are selected, both the male and the female help to build the nest. They choose a site near the edge of the lake and use their bills to push mud and stones into a circular mound twelve to twenty inches tall. The female lays a single egg into a small depression formed in the top of the mound. A circular trench, or moat, carved into the surrounding mud helps protect the nest from rising water. Even with this precaution, rising lake levels during wet years sometimes destroy many flamingo eggs.

Both parents take turns sitting on, or *incubating*, the egg for about a month, at which time the egg hatches. At first, the chick looks nothing like a flamingo! It has a straight pink bill, pink legs, and fluffy gray feathers called *down*. The bill gradually bends as the chick begins to grow, and the chick's feathers—called plumage—eventually change color.

The parents take turns feeding *crop milk* to the chick. The adults produce this rich milk within their digestive systems and pass it to the chick through their bills. The only other bird that produces crop milk is the pigeon.

The flamingo parents care for the chick until it is ready to fly, about seventy-five days after it hatches. By this time the bill has formed a complete bend and the chick is now able to feed itself.

The young flamingo carries its gray plumage for two to three years. Then it slowly begins to grow the bright pink plumage of an adult bird. As the young adult begins to participate in the group displays, it proudly flashes its new colors. Now, it too is capable of finding a mate and raising chicks of its own.

Flamingos, like many other creatures, have very specific habitats within which they can survive. As our human population grows, we are expanding into previously unused areas, forcing animals that live there to adapt, move, or perish. Ever increasing expansion, however, is reducing the amount of suitable habitat to which the animals can move. Some specialized animals such as flamingos simply cannot adapt to new types of habitat.

Because habitat destruction is a leading cause of plant and animal extinctions, we must begin to control our expansion, recognize and preserve critical habitats, and try to minimize our impact on all species.

INDEX

PHOTO RESEARCH
Jim Rothaus / James R. Rothaus & Associates

PHOTO EDITOR
Robert A. Honey / Seattle

PHOTO CREDITS
Len Rue Jr.: front cover,17
Marty Snyderman: 2
COMSTOCK: 4,7,11,13,21,27
Norbert Wu: 8,24,28
COMSTOCK / Sharon Chester: 14
Leonard Lee Rue III: 18
UNICORN STOCK PHOTOS / Robert Christian: 22
UNICORN STOCK PHOTOS / Ron Holt: 31

Library of Congress Cataloging-in-Publication Data
Patton, Don.
Flamingos / Don Patton.
p. cm.
Includes index.
ISBN 1-56766-184-X
(hardcover, reinforced library binding : alk. paper)
1. Flamingos – Juvenile literature
[1. Flamingos.] I. Title.
QL696.C56P38 1995   95-6495
598.3'4 – dc20   CIP
                                          AC